LEAVE NO ONE OUT

My parents didn't believe in 'rules' when my sisters and I were small, and we didn't either. In fact, we might be described as free-range children! There was, however, one absolute, so absolute it didn't seem to be a rule. It was a code of behaviour laid down by my mother, as non-negotiable as a cosmic law. It didn't need to be explained or justified; it couldn't be – it was too fundamental. The law was: leave no one out.

We were fanatical game-players – imaginary games mostly – and often, in a house where large numbers of people would come and go, there were other children around whom we didn't know very well. We and our friends would band together and run off in a raggle-taggle to lark about in the fields and hedgerows, leaving those others behind.

This was my first experience of the universal human urge to club together, to find a sense of identity in a group. I noticed that it was all the more satisfying because there were people who weren't included. The very act of selecting my own friends and having fun with them gave me a sense of superiority. I had the power to invite people into my group, and this sense of power was increased by the knowledge that others secretly felt miserable about being left out.

It was an early experience of an ugliness in humanity – an ugliness we do not grow out of just by becoming adults. Many secular people see 'religion' as the ultimate case of that ugliness. 'Religion,' they think, manifests a dark desire to create and amplify divisions between people. We are all familiar with the idea that 'religion' is a cause of hatred and violence; Richard Dawkins made a TV programme a few years ago with the title, *Religion: The Root of All Evil?*

...... have rounded many well-known modern caring organisations. These include *Shelter, Samaritans, Save the Children, Amnesty International* and the Hospice movement. These are not "Christian organisations" but welcome people of all faiths and none, as volunteers and as clients.

CANON JOHN YOUNG, AUTHOR

Ralph Waldo Emerson, the 19th century American philosopher, deemed beauty to be 'the mark God sets upon virtue'.

'Beauty is the real aspect of things when seen aright and with the eyes of love.'

KATHLEEN RAINE, POET

'If we are not prepared to defend a tolerant society against the onslaught of the intolerant, then the tolerant will be destroyed, and tolerance with them.'

KARL POPPER, PHILOSOPHER

'"Friend," said the Spirit, "could you, only for one moment, fix your mind on something not yourself?"'

C. S. LEWIS, NOVELIST AND APOLOGIST

'Justice is what love looks like in public.'

PROFESSOR CORNEL WEST

'The task of the local church is not just to give Christians opportunity to worship, but to create opportunities for Christians and others to engage in public action.'

ANN MORISY, THEOLOGIAN

'Religious exclusivity boosts trust within the fraternity but engenders an attitude of mistrust to outsiders, as do exclusive clubs such as the Freemasons or Mafia.'

ANTHONY SELDON, EDUCATOR AND HISTORIAN

All too often Christians have confirmed this suspicion. History is littered with examples of Christians behaving as I did with my friends as a child. We create an exclusive identity which makes us feel strong, powerful and 'right'. The word 'Christian' then becomes a weapon of power; it is used to create a mentality of 'us' and 'them'. I don't need to look beyond my own life to see evidence of this.

As we were running away over the fields, I'd brace myself to hear my mother's voice calling after me. I'd walk back, reluctantly, and shamble diffidently over to the ones we had left behind. 'Do you want to come too?' I'd ask. I hated doing it. But it was amazing how, after only a few minutes of playing together, I'd completely forgotten they were once outsiders.

Eventually, my mother didn't have to call out any more because there was a little track that would play in my head: leave no one out.

When Paul writes to the people in Galatia, he is aware that the astonishing news that God loves them might become an excuse for creating a new exclusive club. So he explains, in words so unambiguous it's amazing how easy it's been for Christians to ignore them, that Christian faith is by definition totally inclusive. Why? Because in Christ, *humanity has already achieved complete unity.*

> There is no longer Jew or Greek, there is no longer slave or free, there is no longer male and female; for all of you are one in Christ Jesus.
> (Galatians 3.28)

The writing was on the wall from the first page of the Bible. In humanity, God has drawn a picture of himself. He completed that picture in Christ, in whom God shares our human nature completely. He has united himself definitively with each one of us.

GOD

HAS NO

FAVOURITES

AN ECUMENICAL COURSE
IN 5 SESSIONS

CARMODY GREY

YORK
COURSES

HOW TO GET THE MOST OUT OF THIS COURSE

SUGGESTIONS FOR GROUP LEADERS
We're deliberately not prescriptive, and different leaders prefer to work in slightly different ways, but here are a few tried and trusted ideas . . .

1. **THE ROOM** Encourage people to sit within the main circle – so all feel equally involved.
2. **HOSPITALITY** Tea or coffee and biscuits on arrival and/or at the end of a meeting is always appreciated and encourages people to talk informally.
3. **THE START** If group members don't know one another well, some kind of 'icebreaker' might be helpful. For example, you might invite people to share something about themselves and/or their faith. Be careful to place a time limit on this exercise!
4. **PREPARING THE GROUP** Explain that there are no right or wrong answers, and that among friends it is fine to say things that you're not sure about – to express half-formed ideas. If individuals choose to say nothing, that's all right too.
5. **THE MATERIAL** It helps if each group member has their own personal copy of this booklet. Encourage members to read each session before the meeting. There's no need to consider all the questions. A lively exchange of views is what matters, so be selective. The quotation boxes in the margins are there to stimulate discussion and – just like the opinions expressed by the audio participants – don't necessarily represent York Courses' views or beliefs.
6. **PREPARATION** It's not compulsory for group members to have a Bible, but you will want one. Ask in advance if you want anyone to lead prayers or read aloud, so they can prepare.
7. **TIMING** Aim to start on time and stick fairly closely to your stated finishing time.
8. **USING THE AUDIO** The track markers on the audio (and shown on the transcript) will help you find your way around the recorded material very easily. For each of the sessions we recommend reading through the session in the course booklet, before listening together to the corresponding session on the audio material. Groups may like to choose a question to discuss straight after they have listened to a relevant track on the audio – but there are no hard and fast rules. Do whatever works best for your group!
9. **THE TRANSCRIPT** is a written record of the audio material with track markers for each new question and is invaluable as you prepare. Group members also benefit from having their own copy.

RUNNING A VIRTUAL HOUSE GROUP & SHARING AUDIO ON ZOOM
Various software programmes allow virtual group meetings. Zoom is popular and many people have installed its software already. The group leader should 'host' the meeting (and control the audio element – though this could be taken on by a confident volunteer).

If you have the course CD: Mute everyone else and play the CD as close to your computer microphone as possible.

If your computer has a CD player or you have the downloaded course audio on your computer: At the bottom of the screen click on the 'Share Screen' icon, then at the top of the next screen click on 'Advanced', then click the option 'Music or Computer Sound Only'. The first time you try to share audio you may be asked to 'Install Zoom Audio Device'; follow the instructions to install. Play the audio track on your computer using your preferred media player and everyone will be able to hear it. To stop sharing audio, click 'Stop Share' at the top of the screen.

We suggest group leaders check the audio set-up with a helpful friend before hosting their first virtual meeting.

SESSION 1
THE BEST PICTURE OF GOD

GOD HAS NO FAVOURITES

'Of a truth,' said the banner over St Peter's head in the stained-glass window, 'I perceive that God is no respecter of persons.' It was a warm summer day in my home village in Sussex. Aged perhaps 13, I had ventured down to our local parish church on foot and was alone in the building. Having grown up in a secular family, 'church' was a novel place for me, and Christianity a foreign language. I was looking around for clues as to what this place was for, and what the people who gathered there might think and believe. Craning my head and squinting to see the words in the window against the bright sun coming through, I remember the surprise, the shock even, when I made them out. 'God doesn't respect people?' I thought to myself forlornly. 'Not anyone? No one at all?'

It was an unusual introduction to Christianity. My ideas about it were vague, though I did have a notion that it was basically a welcoming and inclusive faith. However, here I was discovering that God didn't respect people.

The phrase stuck with me and despite the offensive tone, it became oddly precious. It seemed to be saying that this God could not be relied upon to have the same social standards and expectations as everyone else. There was an attractive unpredictability here, and I sensed that I should approach this deity with a certain caution.

Of course, what I saw in the stained glass in my parish church was the wonderful but now rather opaque Authorized (or 'King James') Version of Acts 10.34. As I found my way around the strange phraseology of this translation, it became clearer to me what the text was really saying. God did not have any regard for a

'We do not enter the world with a blank mind – a *tabula rasa* upon which the experiences of our individual life are to be written. We inherit a mind that already has a structure to it. From birth we all tend to think and feel in certain predetermined ways . . . there [is] an evolutionary imprint, but also another imprint – one that I attribute to God. We are truly made in the image of God – the God who created not only the physical world but also our minds.'

DR RUSSELL STANNARD OBE, PROFESSOR EMERITUS OF PHYSICS

'My God is that which rivets my attention, centres my activity, preoccupies my mind, and motivates my action.'

LUKE TIMOTHY JOHNSON, NEW TESTAMENT SCHOLAR

'The great fact for which all religion stands is the confrontation of the human soul with the transcendent holiness of God.'

JOHN BAILLIE, THEOLOGIAN

'Our specifically human existence consists precisely in our hearing the Word of God. We are what we hear from God.'

EMIL BRUNNER, THEOLOGIAN

'God chose to come to us as a man, but did so through the grace and faithfulness of a woman. And in his adult life Jesus rewrote the cultural rule book by treating women with equality and dignity.'

JUSTIN BRIERLEY, THEOLOGIAN

'As Christians we are called to minister where we are.'

STEPHANIE HAYTON, READER

'You look at the human body and you cannot help but just be flabbergasted. Even the fact that each person has a unique set of fingerprints — and the billions of people before us and the billions that are yet to be born will all have individual fingerprints. That is the nature of God, if you like.'

ANNIE LENNOX, SINGER-SONGWRITER

person's position or standing in the world (unlike, say, Lady Catherine de Bourgh in *Pride and Prejudice*). Later, when I learnt New Testament Greek at university, I found more helpful contemporary words: *God has no favourites.*

The full verse explains the significance of this insight. In the Authorized Version's beautiful language, it reads as follows: *Then Peter opened his mouth, and said, Of a truth I perceive that God is no respecter of persons: but in every nation he that feareth him, and worketh righteousness, is accepted with him.*

In Acts 10, Peter has just seen God bless and accept Cornelius, a pagan and a member of the hated oppressing class, a Roman soldier no less. He is recognizing with awe that God's favour, God's *acceptance*, is not meted out according to race or national belonging. To understand this, we need to go back to the very beginning of the Bible, to the start of the whole story.

THE BEST PICTURE OF GOD

A little girl in primary school was working hard on a picture. Her teacher came over asked what she was drawing. 'I'm drawing a picture of God.' 'But no one knows what God looks like,' said the teacher. 'They will in a minute!' came the reply.

The reason this story amuses us is because the absurdity seems so obvious — we know no one can draw a picture of God: God is invisible. Yet we should pause before we rush to laugh at the little girl. The Bible says that God has 'drawn a picture' of himself: us. *God created human beings in his own image. In the image of God he created them* (Genesis 1.27).

The impact of this extraordinary idea is lost on us through familiarity. But if we recover the mind of a child, we can access it anew. We all want to know 'what God looks like', don't we? We all want, like Moses, to 'see' God. Well, the Bible gives us very clear instruction of what to do if so, because each human person, it says, is a picture of God. (I like the word 'picture' instead of the more familiar 'image'. 'Image' sounds rather high-minded and abstract, but we all know a picture when we see one.) This is the pivotal claim made by the Hebrew scriptures about humanity. If we want to know what God 'looks like', we simply need to look at one another.

Of course, we know that God doesn't have a body. The Bible expresses this sense of God's invisibility when it says that *no one can see God* (Timothy 6.16). The opening sections of Genesis, in which the creation of the world is described, make clear that God is not part of his creation. He cannot be, because he is its source. God is invisible, transcendent over all material things. So how can a human being, a little piece of that creation, be a true 'image' or picture of him? Indeed, the Hebrew author of Genesis is so anxious to stress this seemingly bizarre idea that he repeats it twice, as though we might not have believed it the first time round. *In the image of God he created them.*

For the Christian, the meaning and sense of this claim – that every human is a picture of God – is not spelt out fully in the terms of the Hebrew Bible alone. Paul, a Jew soaked in his sacred scriptures, clearly had Genesis 1.27 in mind when he says in his letter to the Colossians that Jesus is *the image of the invisible God*. The ultimate and final picture of God is Jesus. God entered God's creation in the body, heart and life of a human being. He made himself visible; gave himself a definitive image; became a true and reliable picture.

In Eastern Orthodox churches, the interior is filled with 'icons', pictures of the saints. The Orthodox understand that whichever individual saint a particular icon represents, it is always, above all, an image of Christ. Some question the way the Orthodox reverence icons.

Some cafés offer a 'Pay It Forward Scheme' where a future drink can be bought for anyone in need for them to redeem at any time. 'Pay It Forward' is about much more than coffee; it promotes kindness. The pre-paid drink may be claimed by anyone in need.

'I have no visual image of God, so a picture of God is not how I perceive the Almighty. Growing up with the assurance that we were made in God's image was some kind of comfort. I don't see God as a humanoid with two arms and two legs and two eyes and so forth, more a reassuring father-like presence. I live in hope that I will recognize God's presence when the ultimate comes along.'

J. GILMOUR, CHRISTIAN

'Understanding that Jesus Christ dying for my sins spoke to the humility we all have to have as human beings – that we're sinful and we're flawed and we make mistakes, and that we achieve salvation through the grace of God. But what we can do, as flawed as we are, is still see God in other people, and do our best to help them find their own grace.'

BARACK OBAMA,
44TH PRESIDENT OF THE USA

'As Paul stresses again and again, God's love is shown in Christ's redemptive sacrifice on the Cross, through which our lives can be transformed. By demonstrating kindness ourselves, we can show Christ's love for the world, a love which is reverence for the unique quality of each and every human being and each and every life form.'

MARGARET IVES, READER

But it is God, in Christ, who they are venerating in the icon of a human person, because a human being is, for them, as for the author of Genesis, a picture of God. 'The saints' are those in whom this picture is especially visible or obvious.

Every human is a picture of God, and Jesus is the ultimate picture in which those other images come into focus. In Jesus, humanness is revealed to be sacred – not just because God cares for it, but because God shows the depth of his own being and his own love in the form of a human person.

ICONS IN THE DUSTBIN

There are daunting consequences of this way of thinking about human beings, which Jesus himself spells out. He does this most vividly in the famous 'parable of the sheep and the goats' (Matthew 25.31–46), explaining that whatever we do, or fail to do, to any human, we are doing or failing to do to *him*. God is completely identified with every human individual. In the wonderful words of the Second Vatican Council: *'In the Incarnation, God has united himself definitively with every human being.'* The apostle John draws the inescapable conclusion from this: *If you say you love God, but you hate your brother, you are a liar* (1 John 4.20).

After knowing Jesus, we simply cannot separate the way we treat any person from our relationship to him. He advises us very directly: if we want to know the quality of our relationship with Jesus, we need simply look at the quality of our relationships with other human beings.

This seems demanding enough but there is more. Jesus is concerned to explain in this parable that it is the poor, the sick, the hungry, the thirsty, the naked and the imprisoned with whom he is especially identified. These categories are not supposed to be exhaustive. Jesus is identified with anyone who is suffering, who has been hurt, neglected or wounded – including those we think may 'deserve' it (such as, we might suppose, those in prison). In other words, he is most strongly identified with those whose sacredness is probably the hardest for us to recognize. It is our attitude towards broken people that is the ultimate test of our relationship with Jesus.

There's a story about a modern Greek Orthodox saint who used to work with prostitutes. Some of his fellow believers were disapproving. They felt that by ministering among such people, without judgement, he was somehow licensing their lifestyle. (I do not know which Bible they were reading!) At some point the saint, goaded by attacks that he was encouraging sin, reportedly responded to his critics with the words: 'When I look at these women, I do not see sinners. I see icons in the dustbin.'

To 'deface' something is, literally, to take away its face; to spoil, blemish or disfigure it. God in Jesus has given himself forever a human face. When the dignity of a human being is compromised, through poverty, exclusion, discrimination, violence, or diminishment of any kind, God himself has been 'defaced'.

People who have suffered in this way are 'icons in the dustbin'. Instead of being venerated as windows into the divine, they have ended up in the rubbish. An old-fashioned term for this is 'blasphemy': taking what is holy – God – and making it unholy.

Christianity offers us a definitive description of a human being: every one of us is a picture of God. And it issues one devastatingly simple instruction: every human is to be treated as though they were Christ, because in a very real way, they are. *Whatever you do to the least of these, you do to me.*

'If we are going to offer hospitality – which means tea and coffee after the service – let it be good coffee and good tea. And if there's going to be biscuits, let them not bend when you lift them out of the tin, because they've been lying in some mouldy cupboard for the past seven days. I mean that's a bad witness to the gospel.'

JOHN BELL, HYMN WRITER AND BROADCASTER

THE BEST PICTURE OF GOD

Some groups will address all the questions. That's fine. Others prefer to select just a few and spend longer on each. That's fine, too. Horses for (York) Courses!

1. If you had to draw a picture of God, what would it look like? Do you find an inability to visualize God a hindrance to believing in him?

2. Revisit Track 2 of the course audio/transcript. Have you ever felt as though you are less important to God than other people?

3. On p. 3 of the course booklet, Carmody writes that 'each human person is a picture of God' and that 'if we want to know what God "looks like", we simply need to look at one another'. How do you see God in others?

4. Revisit Track 5. According to Carmody (on p. 5), 'It is our attitude towards broken people that is the ultimate test of our relationship with Jesus.' Who are the vulnerable, excluded and denigrated people in your personal life? Your work life? Your leisure and wider pursuits?

5. Reread the story about the modern Greek Orthodox saint on p. 5. Do you feel his work would arouse the same level of disapproval in your church in 2021? What do you feel causes disapproval in your church?

6. Revisit p. 2 and Track 5. Peter struggled to accept that Cornelius, a pagan, was acceptable to God. Which person or group of people do you struggle to see as loved by God? Do you find that 'Christ and the Spirit do in us what we're not capable of doing'?

7. On Track 4 'wrestling with the Bible' is discussed. How significant is the Bible to your faith? Does the Bible ever hinder/detract from your faith/belief?

8. On Track 5 Jim describes the teaching that 'we should treat others as we would wish to be treated' as the 'golden rule'. Do you agree? What is your own 'golden rule' from Christianity/your faith?

9. Carmody grew up in a secular family. Yet she is now an active Christian. Reflect on your own journey into faith and share it with other group members. (Note: group members are invited to offer reflections and ask questions when others are explaining their own 'journey'.)

10. Her local church raised questions for young Carmody. Has a building (secular or sacred) ever done this for you?

In Christ, God is telling us the most important thing about himself: he leaves nobody out. This is what the apostle John means when he says that God is love (1 John 4.8). Love is, in fact, *what God is*.

We, who have obscured the picture of God in us with the desire to divide and exclude that which the Bible calls 'sin', find 'identity' by placing ourselves over against one another. We are this; *they* are that. God does not share that ugliness, the ugliness that seeks to divide. God does not shore up his own identity by denigrating others. He cannot, because God's identity is 'love': unlimited welcome; unrestricted acceptance; total embrace.

This is the only way God can be, because God is the source and destiny of all things. That's what we mean when we say that God is 'Creator'. There is nothing that is outside God. The rule of my childhood really was an absolute law: the law of God.

EVERYONE IS CHOSEN

One of the rituals performed by the Pope each Easter is 'the washing of the feet' on Maundy Thursday. Along with priests and bishops all over the world, the Pope washes the feet of 12 people to re-enact Jesus' washing of his disciples' feet on the evening of the Last Supper. At his first Easter as Pope, Francis washed the feet of some inmates of one of Rome's more notorious prisons. A few of them were Muslims.

Some Catholics were outraged. Surely, they thought, the point of the washing of the feet is that those men are disciples of Jesus, that is, 'Christians'. They said that Pope Francis had destroyed the deep symbolism of the act by washing the feet of people from another religion.

It's easy enough to understand their discomfort. Usually, religious rituals confirm the identity of those inside,

'There's the Ignatian saying, "Give me a 7-year-old, and I'll show you the adult . . ." If people experience church in their early years as something that's for other people but not them, we have a mountain to climb later in showing that they're part of God's People.'

THE REVD DR SHARON MOUGHTIN-MUMBY

'We must learn to see beyond colour and recognize the giftings in one another. We should celebrate each other because all that we have here on earth is given to us by God, and what is paramount to him is the true love that we share. Sincere love is for all and not selective. It reaches out to the lonely and the unnoticed. True love says: "I see you and love you with the love of Christ just as you are."'

FUNMI MAKANJU, LICENSED LAY MINISTER

and separate them more clearly from those outside. Unfortunately for those who seek this kind of security, which includes all of us on some level, Jesus practised no such discrimination. He did not confirm and reinforce the religious divides of his own time. He broke them down.

The most fundamental divide in the world Jesus inhabited was that between 'Jew' and 'Gentile'. To be a Jew was to be a member of Israel, God's people; a chosen one. To be a 'Gentile' was to be a member of 'the nations'; that is, everyone else.

Jesus, himself a Jew, breaks down this wall from within. Paul is at great pains to emphasize this in many of his letters. The distinction between Jew and Gentile is no longer relevant. This is the meaning of his claim, which seems a little arcane to us, that Gentiles do not need to be circumcised to become Christians. His point is that the divide between Jew and Gentile is now out of date. Belonging to Jesus gives a person an identity deeper, more all-encompassing than any ethnic, cultural or religious grouping. Paul urged Jews and Gentiles to abandon their 'us' and 'them' mentality.

It's easy for us to underestimate how profoundly challenging this would have been for Paul's readers. The distinction between Jew and Gentile was the fundamental distinction in Paul's own life. He himself had been a Pharisee, for whom the observance of Israel's law set the Jews completely apart from 'the nations', that is, those around them. Paul, reflecting on the significance of Jesus, finds himself forced to abandon the great binary that had once shaped his identity. Now, *there is neither Jew nor Gentile*. The oneness of humanity in Christ has erased that divide. In Christ, everyone is 'chosen' – *chosen from before the foundation of the world* (Ephesians 1.4).

We might feel that the distinction between Jew and Gentile is not relevant to us, since by and large we do not think in terms of these categories. But we are very familiar with the opposition that exists between faith identities. We know that they are a source of tension, conflict and violence in many parts of the world. In all societies, including our own, groups of people are categorized and opposed according to their beliefs. 'Secularists' versus 'religious' people; atheists versus believers; Christians versus Muslims; Catholics versus Protestants, and so on. We love these labels and never get tired of attaching them to ourselves and others.

But Paul tells us, simply and directly, that the unity of humanity in Christ is deeper than all political, cultural and religious separation.

THE COMPANY OF JESUS

Being with Jesus is being in the company of someone who accepted people of 'all nations', all ethnicities, all religions. It's not comfortable company! As I discovered in my childhood games, we love to form our own groups, and gain a special sense of security when we can leave others out of them. There is something satisfying about running off with our own friends, the like-minded, those we agree with, who reinforce our sense of specialness over against everyone else. In the grown-up world, 'religion' (or the rejection of it) is one of the prime ways we do this.

But Jesus calls out after us with words we so often don't want to hear: leave no one out. He asks us to walk back, approach those we have excluded, and say: 'Do you want to come too?'

In fact, the only people Jesus was really angry with were those who used 'God' to exclude or diminish others. For Jesus, this was the sole disqualification of being with him: that we use our chosenness to make others seem un-chosen. That is what we do when we use 'Christianity' to diminish the identity of others.

'People are already organized into networks, interest groups, even power blocs. It is a highly contested cultural landscape, not a wilderness.'

MARGARET PICKUP, AUTHOR

'Be hospitable to one another without complaining.'

1 PETER 4.9

Being willing to include everyone – even those we don't agree with, who belong to a different group from ourselves, and who we perhaps think are not worthy of our company and attention – is the one and only 'rule' for those who want to be with Jesus. If you want to be with him, you need to be with everyone. Because in Christ, humanity is one.

SESSION 2
NEITHER JEW NOR GENTILE

1. On Track 6 of the course audio/transcript, Carmody says that 'leave no one out' is the keynote of Christianity. Have you ever experienced the feeling of being left out? Can you think of a time you and your friends excluded someone else? Has this ever happened in a church setting?

2. On p. 8, Carmody writes that the word 'Christian' can become a weapon of power used to create a mentality of 'us' and 'them'. Do you agree? Is this something of which you have personal experience?

3. Revisit Track 7. Do you agree that in order for people to belong, they need to be missed? What is the mix within your church – is any one sector of society under-represented?

4. On p. 11 (para headed The Company of Jesus), Carmody writes about being willing to include everyone – even those we don't agree with. Do you believe this is a fundamental rule for being with Jesus? How hard or easy do you – and/or your church – find this to do?

5. Track 9. Does – or should – the Church have a part to play in trying/helping to heal the wounds left by the divide in this country over Brexit?

6. Reread Mike Kelly's words on p. 10 ('Young people are desperate for community and belonging. That's why they like social media; it gives them the opportunity to stay connected with their communities and be present even if they are not there.') Do you agree? If so, are there other groups of people who are desperate for community and belonging in your view?

7. Revisit Track 8 where Carmody talks about the ways in which the church succeeds and read John Young's words on p. 7 (about Shelter & Amnesty). What does your church do that inspires you and makes you proud to belong? Can you think of examples of love/self-sacrifice you've experienced?

8. The only people Jesus was really angry with were those who used 'God' to exclude or diminish others. Are there patterns of exclusion in your own Christian community?

9. Revisit Track 7 (about Charles de Foucauld). What makes you want to be part of the church?

10. What might be some equivalents, in our own society, of the divide in Paul's world between 'Jew' and 'Gentile'?

'Gender inequalities have also been put front and centre by the [Covid] pandemic. The Office of National Statistics found that women took on the bulk of childcare in the home during lockdown, while the campaign #ButNotMaternity highlighted the discrepancies in restrictions that allowed the public to go to the pub or fly abroad, while pregnant women faced a lot of their maternity services — including scans, and sometimes even the birth — alone. It's noticeable that many of the people we see campaigning are women. "It is probably because they are not as well-served by the establishment, which is still male-dominated," says Helen Pankhurst, who is gender advisor at the charity CARE International. "And you either accept the status quo or you rise. I think we are seeing that rising."'

ANNA BONET, JOURNALIST

'MAN' AND 'HUMANITY'

'One small step for a man,' as Neil Armstrong believed he said as he stepped off the Apollo moon lander, 'one giant leap for mankind.' Like everyone else of my generation, I innocently inherited that ambiguous term: when referring to all human beings, I habitually use 'mankind', with its obvious implication that 'man' is the standard and norm, and 'woman' at best a sort of variation.

I always rather liked 'man' and 'mankind'. They had a sort of grandeur and dignity about them. So I was offended when my tutors at university started circling the terms in red pen when I put them into my essays. They asked me to use the cumbersome 'humanity' instead.

I tried to defend 'mankind', saying that 'humanity' had too many syllables. It lacked gravitas. But when I thought about it, I reluctantly had to concede their point. Using a term that implies maleness is normative humanity, and femaleness a deviation from it, was indefensible. If 'man' indicated 'all of us', then men were the real humans, women just a variant.

In the world Paul came from, that assumption was standard. No less an individual than the founder of Western philosophy, Socrates, was said to have thanked the gods 'that I was born a human and not a beast; a man and not a woman; a Greek and not a barbarian'. A similar sentiment found its way into the Jewish prayer-book, which proposes as one of the daily prayers: 'Blessed are you O God, King of the Universe, Who has not made me a Gentile, a slave, or a woman.' This kind of thinking was dominant in both the cultures in which, and to which, Paul's letters were written — the Jewish and the Greek. In these societies, being 'male' or 'female' was not incidental. It determined your public role, your economic and social standing, your opportunities and your freedoms.

In some ways the twenty-first century has moved on from the prejudices of those ancient societies, but in many ways, it hasn't. Misogyny is one of the universal common denominators of humanity. In Western societies, modern media culture has generated expectations of youth, beauty and physical perfection which place extreme pressure on women of all ages. Globally, women still have fewer opportunities for economic participation than men. They have poorer access to education. They face greater health and safety risks in their daily lives. And they have lower levels of political representation. For most women in our world, being female is still a terrible disadvantage. Across huge swathes of our globe, you are still likely to thank God for being born male, and lament being born female.

My parents sent me and my two sisters to a school famous for being the first co-educational boarding establishment in this country. There we had a humorous saying: as a girl, you can do everything the boys can do, and most things better. It was only a turn of phrase, but it communicated a certain spirit, a quality of boldness and defiance. If I wanted, if I chose, the sky was the limit for me as a girl. I knew I could be exceptional.

When, as a young adult, I approached Christian communities for the first time, I was shocked and baffled to encounter what often seemed an opposite view. Women in the churches appeared routinely unable to express their gifts, or receive recognition for their contribution; they seemed confined by social roles that diminished them. Far from giving women refuge from the pressures their societies placed on them, churches often appeared to reinforce those pressures. My secular peers viewed them as representing a repressive past which

'Sure Fred Astaire was great, but don't forget that Ginger Rogers did everything he did . . . backwards and in high heels.'

BOB THAVES, CARTOONIST

'There are no right answers to wrong questions.'

URSULA K. LE GUIN, AUTHOR

'I myself have never been able to find out precisely what feminism is: I only know that people call me a feminist whenever I express sentiments that differentiate me from a doormat.'

REBECCA WEST, WRITER

'Men are afraid that women will laugh at them. Women are afraid that men will kill them.'

MARGARET ATWOOD, WRITER

'Remember that you are an Englishman, and have consequently won first prize in the lottery of life.'

CECIL RHODES, 19TH CENTURY BRITISH IMPERIALIST

'As women, we know that being a Christian means we have joined a predominantly androcentric and patricentric story. Christianity was founded on Jesus and the twelve male apostles. It was recorded by men, has been interpreted and transmitted mostly by men, and passed down through institutions led by men. Finding our place in that requires a bit more imagination and searching than it does for men!'

**DR LUCY PEPPIATT,
THEOLOGIAN**

'I ask no favour for my sex. All I ask of our brethren is that they take their feet off our necks.'

**SARAH MOORE GRIMKÉ,
19TH CENTURY AMERICAN
ABOLITIONIST**

'Women will have achieved true equality when men share with them the responsibility of bringing up the next generation.'

**RUTH BADER GINSBURG,
ASSOCIATE JUSTICE OF THE U.S.
SUPREME COURT**

'Without affirmation it is hard to live well.'

**HENRI NOUWEN, DUTCH
CATHOLIC PRIEST**

modern and open societies should want to leave behind. I didn't know how to defend these communities to the wider, sceptical secular world. Groups which campaign for women's rights so often see the churches as enemies, and it was hard to argue with them.

THE IDENTITY WARS

'Masculinity' and 'femininity' are war zones in contemporary culture. Gender has become contested and painful territory, in which people's identity and self-worth are bitterly fought over. What is it to be a woman? To be a man? How should the two relate to each other? Addressing these questions in the public space is taking one's life in one's hands: the issue is so divisive, so sensitive, it seems better to stay silent on the subject.

Frequently, the Bible is seen as delivering a single clear message in this conversation. There are two genders, male and female, with different roles, purposes and identities in God's plan. Paul in some ways provides ammunition for this kind of perception, with his well-known instruction on the roles of wives and husbands (e.g. Ephesians 5.22–5). But the most important text which is thought to support this view is the archetypal description of the image of God in Genesis: *In the image of God he created them; male and female he created them.*

Many people worry that defining particular identities and roles, based on a person's gender, results in confining people in categories that, in reality, are appropriate for only a few. When women or men in traditional societies fail to fit those traditional categories, they are often ostracized and excluded. Those who are transgender – people who cross the biological and social boundaries between 'male' and 'female' – face particular persecution in many parts of the world.

Paul was a faithful and dedicated reader of his Scriptures. His Jewish Bible or 'Torah' comprised the first five books of what we know as the Old Testament, beginning with Genesis. The Genesis statement about the nature of human beings would have been second nature to him: God made human beings male and female. Two types, two categories of humanity. The two types are even given discernibly different roles in Genesis; woman is to be man's 'helpmate', as the old version has it.

How unexpected, then, that when Paul is thinking through the meaning of Christ in his letter to the Galatians, he seems to throw all that out of the window. *In Christ*, he says, *there is no longer male and female* (Galatians 3.28). Paul's experience of Christ makes him reassess the way of thinking about gender his society took for granted.

CHRIST: THE ONLY IDENTITY THAT MATTERS

What we call 'the New Testament' is really 'the new testimony'; that is to say, 'the new witness'. A witness, or testimony, results from someone having seen something and being able to report on it directly, in a first-person way. In the 'new witness' that we call the New Testament, the authors are reacting to having seen something that shattered existing categories of thought. That 'something' is Christ. Having seen Christ, having known and encountered Christ, the authors find themselves having to rethink the concepts and frameworks they had received from their past, whether Jewish or Greek.

Paul is gripped by the conviction that in the person of Jesus, humanity is revealed for what it most deeply is. In this face, in this body, in this life, we know at last what it is to be a human being. To quote the Second Vatican Council once more: '*Christ reveals humanity to*

'Representation of the world, like the world itself, is the work of men; they describe it from their own point of view, which they confuse with absolute truth.'

SIMONE DE BEAUVOIR, WRITER

'The scriptures have also been used to undermine black beauty. In the Old Testament, for instance, only a few of the modern translations of the Song of Solomon replace the *less obvious* conjunctive 'but' with the more *commonly acceptable* 'and' so that the Song begins with an affirmation of the female subject. Translated accurately she is "dark and beautiful."'

PROFESSOR ROBERT BECKFORD

'Organized Christianity has probably done more to retard the ideals that were its founders than any other agency in the world.'

RICHARD LE GALLIENNE, WRITER

'Female biology is not the reason women are the bum-wiping class. But recognising a child as female is the reason she will be brought up to expect and accept that as her role. Recognising a woman as female is the reason she will be seen as the appropriate person to clear up after everyone in the office.'

'Women make up just 13% of the main subject of global media stories; only 28% of speaking roles in Hollywood films are female; out of 47 topics in Key Stage 3 of the national history curriculum, only one topic mentions women, while Key Stage 2's 34 topics have room for only three women's names. Wherever we look, our culture is ignoring women.'

CAROLINE CRIADO PEREZ, AUTHOR OF *INVISIBLE WOMEN*

itself.' When Paul says that in Christ there is no male and female, he is rethinking the old, familiar categories in the light of the astonishing new reality he has encountered in the carpenter from Nazareth. Christ, Paul says, is not just the revelation of God, but the revelation of humanness. Christ shows us to ourselves. In his life, we find out *what it is to be human*. In Galatians 3.28, Paul is expressing with crystalline clarity this fundamental insight: that in Jesus he has discovered the deep truth of *every single human being*.

The most profound human difference is that created by our gendered bodies. It is this difference that is recorded in Genesis as the fundamental distinction between human beings. But, Paul is saying, even this most important difference is superficial, compared to the deepest and truest identity of each one of us. What defines us as human beings is not our gender; it is not our culture; it is not our religion or our race. No, the identity that ultimately defines us as human beings is Christ. This is what Paul means when he describes Christ as the final and ultimate 'Adam': the real and true human being (1 Corinthians 15.45). In Christ we finally see what the meaning of the 'first Adam' – the archetype of humanity – was all along.

Paul is not naïve. He realizes, of course, that 'maleness' and 'femaleness' have commonly understood meanings in our physical and cultural worlds, just as Jewishness and non-Jewishness, freedom and slavery, are real categories in the real world.

The point Paul is making is that this 'real world' is not, actually, the *most* real world. It is not the only level on which Christians should operate. In fact, it is not even the *primary* level on which Christians should operate. The basic lens through which Christians are to see all humans is Christ. It is through Christ that we see the *most real* world. Through Christ, we perceive the most fundamental identity of each person.

This identity is the absolute basic gift of our existence as human beings. What is that identity? Simply, being loved by God, adopted by God, lifted up and embraced by God. This is what it is to be human.

In this identity, there is no opposition, no division, no parting of ways around gender, race, religion or culture. In Christ we do not belong to different groups which set us over against one another. In Christ, there is simply the truth of our common origin – we are all children of God – and our common destiny – we are all heirs to the kingdom of heaven.

'When General Synod voted for women to be admitted to the office of an ordained priest, it represented a *huge* step forward for the Church and released fantastic amounts of unique ministry. Women bring all that women bring, and men bring all that men bring and the whole experience for the Church is so much richer. Why wouldn't we want that?'

B. BURBRIDGE, CHRISTIAN

'If you believe that everyone should play by the same rules and be judged by the same standards, that would have got you labelled a radical 50 years ago, a liberal 25 years ago, and a racist today.'

THOMAS SOWELL, SOCIAL THEORIST

SESSION 3
NEITHER MALE NOR FEMALE

1. On p. 15, Carmody writes about women in the churches appearing confined by social roles that diminish them. Do you feel this is true of your church? (What is the ratio of women to men on your church's coffee rota??)

2. Revisit Track 12 of the course audio/transcript. How close are women coming to having equal status and full parity with men in the church, in your view?

3. When you first heard a woman preaching, or received the Sacrament from a woman's hands, how did you feel?

4. In Genesis, God makes human beings, with their gendered bodies, in the divine image. But gender differences have often been used to exclude and discriminate. How do you experience gender difference in your culture?

5. Read Galatians 3.28: *In Christ there is no male and female.* How do you think Jesus would have felt about transgender people? Do you feel the same way?

6. Revisit Track 12 and the words of the 19th century British imperialist Cecil Rhodes on p. 15. ('Remember that you are an Englishman, and have consequently won first prize in the lottery of life.') Can you think of people/ organizations who still embrace this kind of thinking? Discuss!

7. On p. 17, Carmody writes 'Paul is gripped by the conviction that in the person Jesus, humanity is revealed for what it most deeply is. In this face, in this body, in this life, we know at last what it is to be a human being.' Do these words resonate with you? To what extent does your Christian faith help you see who you really are in Christ?

8. Track 10. How do you feel about the changes to language in services over the past few decades? Do you miss the use of 'Thees' and 'Thous'? How about the introduction of gender-neutral language, such as 'humanity' rather than 'mankind'?

9. Track 13. According to Carmody on p. 18, 'the most profound human difference is that created by our gendered bodies'. Do you agree? These days gender is a hot topic for discussion. Might society be more equal if humans were no longer identified by/categorized by their gender?

10. Are non-believers also children of God? How about people who know nothing of the Christian story?

SESSION 4
NEITHER SLAVE NOR FREE

A BROKEN WORLD

Driven by my Dad's work as a photojournalist, our family travelled a lot when I was a child. A few decades ago, the world was much less globalized and connected than it is now, and we regularly visited places 'tourism' had not reached. Often, these visits were uplifting and transformative, filled with light and colour, showing me astonishing realities I couldn't have imagined. The joy and wonder of those experiences gave me vision and purpose and shaped my thoughts of what life was about.

But my childhood travels also introduced a troubled sense that all was not well with the world. Memories of faces marked by pain, difficulty, hopelessness. Fragile bodies, old before their time, crippled by back-breaking work, malnutrition and lack of access to medical care. The terrifying sight of the ill and the aged. Stultifying, dangerous, monotonous labour, with no sick pay, no pension, no healthcare. Instead, the constant threat of food shortage, illness, disability, homelessness, violence. And worst of all, no alternative. No rescue. No exit.

The most vivid of these unsettling encounters took place in Bangladesh in 1990, where the slowly increasing trickle of travellers from the West was bolstering the popularity of begging on the streets. Adults in the trade would deliberately mutilate children – sometimes their own offspring – to make their begging more effective.

Our friends, who worked in development, told us not to give money to those beggars, lest we encourage this appalling practice. Walking past children as they sat on the street, sometimes blind, sometimes with limbs amputated, was one of the hardest things I've ever had to do. The sight was so wretched, it almost broke your heart. But perhaps the worst part was imagining the

'Surely an all-powerful God would be able to end suffering, and a good God would want to. The problem here is that suffering is only a challenge once you already believe in such a God. For an atheist, bad stuff just happens, and you've got nobody you can complain to.'

ADRIAN ROBERTS, READER IN LEEDS DIOCESE AND AUTHOR

'The spirit of God would seem to be inviting the development of a more humble, vulnerable, popular style of Christian community that is less hierarchical and more from the roots, is of the people more than it is for the people.'

CANON ROBIN GREENWOOD

'What characterises all the wealthy is their lack of contentment – and this at the expense of others.'

BRUCE MALINA, BIBLE SCHOLAR

'Unlike Peter Mandelson, the Bible is not intensely relaxed about people getting filthy rich.'

THE REVD DR GILES FRASER

'The only good life is one in which there is no need for miracles.'

NADEZHDA MANDELSTAM, WRITER AND EDUCATOR

'The task of prophetic ministry is to nurture, nourish and evoke a consciousness and perception alternative to that of the dominant culture around us.'

WALTER BRUEGGEMANN, OLD TESTAMENT SCHOLAR & THEOLOGIAN

despair of parents who felt driven to do such dreadful things to their children. Walking on, leaving them behind in their hopelessness, felt like a terrible act of betrayal. Looking into the face of their need and their anguish, yet knowing that safety and comfort awaited me when I returned home, was a moral contradiction I didn't know how to live with.

I still don't. And the fact that those people are far away and not on our doorstep doesn't change a thing.

THE SCANDAL OF THE GOSPEL

Christianity came into a world in which gross, tortuous inequality was not considered tragic. It was not called into question. It was simply the way the world was. There was nothing particularly to be said or done about it, no objection to be made.

Some people were slaves. They had no opportunities, no rights, no dignity, and no future of their own. Owners could do anything – literally anything – to their slaves, and no one could contest that. Some people were free, through no personal merit. And some were not only free but citizens, with rights to public respect, political representation and justice.

This was simply the universe as it was in the ancient world. No one expected or looked for anything different.

The gospel broke into this stratified, hierarchical and fixed order of things like an earthquake. Jesus scandalized those around him by acting as though every human being mattered. His behaviour threw into profound question the basic political arrangements of Roman and Greek societies and was viewed by the authorities as a serious threat. Jesus undermined the whole order of society, in which rich and poor, slave and free, knew their places. The stability of the state depended on the quiet acceptance of this arrangement. Jesus' alternative – radical inclusion of everyone, without respect to wealth, birth, gender or race – seemed dangerous and destabilising.

The early Christians too were attached to the old order, in which people accepted where life put them, and nothing was unsettled or out of place. They liked the conventional ways, which told people who to sit with, what to wear, who spoke and who was spoken to, who gave orders and who took them.

But as James explained to his community in Jerusalem, any attempt to maintain social boundaries after Jesus is unsustainable.

> For if a person with gold rings and in fine clothes comes into your assembly, and if a poor person in dirty clothes also comes in, and if you take notice of the one wearing the fine clothes and say, 'Have a seat here, please,' while to the one who is poor you say, 'Stand there,' or, 'Sit at my feet,' have you not made distinctions among yourselves . . ? (James 2.2–4)

'Have you not made distinctions among yourselves?' In other words, have you not made societal boundaries too real, too important? James calls a spade a spade. Behaviour like this is simply 'favouritism'. Preferential treatment. In our language: discrimination. He puts a hard question to those who conduct themselves in this way: *Do you with your acts of favouritism really believe in our glorious Lord Jesus Christ?* (James 2.1).

This is an odd question. Why would favouritism be in tension with 'believing in our glorious Lord Jesus Christ'?

The 'glory' of Christ is his beauty. This beauty is a sharing without limit, without discrimination. Preferential treatment – 'discrimination' – destroys this beauty. It is, literally, incompatible with it.

'All our hope of knowing ourselves is in knowing other people.'

ROSEMARY HAUGHTON, THEOLOGIAN

'A Christian is someone who shares the sufferings of God in the world.'

DIETRICH BONHOEFFER, GERMAN PASTOR

'The message of Christ is that God is found in vulnerability, amongst the maligned and despised. Christians are called to take up the invitation to create communities where all people, including Black and Minority Ethnic people can flourish. And in my mind, such flourishing is about being free to be oneself, being free to live and breathe in black and brown skins.'

THE REVD DR CATHERINE OKORONKWO

IN OUR TIME

Bruce Longenecker's book *Lost Letters of Pergamum* imagines what it would have felt like for a Roman citizen to join the Christian community in the generation after Jesus. In the new sort of society that the followers of Jesus created, a Roman citizen's special, exclusive citizenship – which guaranteed him (and it was always a *him*) rights to representation, justice and public dignity – was now insignificant. It faded into irrelevance, in comparison with the new citizenship shared by everyone in the community: the citizenship of heaven (Philippians 3.20).

Lost Letters of Pergamum chronicles the journey of Antipas, a Roman citizen, who makes the reluctant decision to join the community of those who follow the carpenter from Nazareth. In that community, he discovers that he loves and cares for a man who, in his own world, is a nobody: a mere slave. Antipas learns to see that this slave, this nobody, is really a somebody – a three-dimensional person with his own life, his own cares, concerns, interests, fears and dreams. He slowly accepts, and finally rejoices in, the full humanity of this 'slave', equal to his own, even though the state does not recognize it.

We, who live in a less obviously stratified society than Antipas, might think we have already taken this journey; that James' accusation of favouritism doesn't apply to us. But in the twenty-first century, we are still captive to economic and social discrimination. Opportunities to sustain a basic level of dignity, health and security are unevenly distributed even in the UK, which has one of the oldest welfare states in the world. We quietly accept the hierarchies, some implicit and others explicit, in which our culture organizes social groups. Hierarchies of wealth and education; hierarchies of beauty and health; hierarchies of social success and public standing.

Dark places of loss and anguish are so easy to turn away from. What lies behind this turning-away is not malice. It is simply that we look the other way so that we do not see the places of suffering, abandonment and despair.

The shape of contemporary society, in which individuals and families are too often caught up in their own concerns, make it easy for us not to notice the manner in which such hierarchies undermine, diminish and exclude.

GOING TO THE PERIPHERIES

When I met those mutilated children on the streets in Bangladesh, it was hard not to see them. But when I went home I buried the horrible memory under the normality of life. Like the Pharisee, we pass by the wounded man on the other side of the road, because we have things to do, places to go, and no time to waste.

There are what Pope Francis calls 'the peripheries': the edges of our world. These are not only geographical edges, but also social, economic and spiritual margins. In such peripheries there dwell, in Francis' words, 'the vast ranks of the excluded': those who have been left behind, shut out.

In the famous hymn of Philippians, Paul says that Christ, having been a royal ruler, one with the God of the universe, became a *doulos*, literally, a slave. In the new world that is Christ, to be poor, to be without freedoms, is no longer taboo. Christ joined the vast ranks of the excluded. He went to the peripheries.

Those who follow him are asked to go there too.

'We desperately need to see in the mirror of another's eyes our own goodness and beauty, if we are to be truly free.'

JOHN POWELL, JESUIT PRIEST

'Christian celebrity culture is fundamentally against God culture. It encourages the few to believe that they are valuable and the many to believe they are less so.'

KATHARINE WELBY-ROBERTS, APOLOGIST

SESSION 4
NEITHER SLAVE NOR FREE

1. Track 14 of the course audio/transcript. How do you react when you encounter someone begging on the street? Does it make a difference if you are abroad, rather than in your home country?

2. Discipleship is costly, although sometimes the cost relates not to large dramatic gestures but small, often unnoticed, actions. Share examples of 'costly' ways in which you attempt to live out your faith. (Cost can be evaluated in all sorts of ways, including financial and emotional.)

3. 'The glory of God is a person fully alive' according to the 2nd century theologian, Irenaeus. Can you think of someone you know who seems 'fully alive'?

4. Revisit Track 15 and p. 24 where Carmody lists hierarchies in the UK's stratified society. Can you add any others? Do you feel that the Coronavirus pandemic has brought any differences to the fore between how the government/ society treats the old and the young?

5. Read James 2.1–4. Is it always wrong to 'make distinctions among yourselves'? Should we be deferential in the presence of Royalty, as tradition dictates? During the pandemic, NHS staff were prioritized to receive their Covid vaccinations. Do you think government ministers should also have been fast-tracked to get their jabs, to help keep them safe whilst running a country in crisis?

6. Track 17. What is your experience of venturing to 'the peripheries'? How do you respond to those begging for help? (Do you offer hot drinks, chocolate bars, money . . ?) Read about the Pay It Forward scheme on p. 3 – is this something you or your church could be involved in?

7. On Track 16, Frances talks about people who are wealthy being encouraged in the church, 'whereas somebody in dirty clothes, who is poor – what can they bring, but dependency?' What have your own experiences been?

8. Revisit Carmody's and Bernadette's comments on Track 17 and Walter Brueggemann's words on p. 22 ('The task of prophetic ministry is to nurture, nourish and evoke a consciousness and perception alternative to that of the dominant culture around us.') Do you agree?

9. Slavery is not only a past reality, but also a present one. What forms of slavery are there in our world today? Are they visible to you?

SESSION 5
WHAT IS A CHRISTIAN?

CHRISTIAN IDENTITY

Brother Roger of Taizé used to say that Jesus did not come to found a religion. He came to give people life.

We might be suspicious of this. Surely 'Christianity' is a religion? In fact, the word 'Christianity' does not appear in the Bible at all, and the word 'Christian' only three times (Acts 11.26; Acts 26.28; 1 Peter 4.16). The early followers of Jesus were simply known as 'People of the Way'.

Which way? The 'way' that is Jesus (John 14.6). 'People of the Way' are those who start out on a journey, a journey which they follow in large part by inviting others to join them. It is a journey towards life, a full and complete life (John 10.10). That life is distinguished by the fact that it is one of unrestricted sharing; what Paul calls 'fellowship', or communion. This sharing is the very way of Jesus; it is how we travel with him.

Sometimes I think we should drop the word 'Christianity' altogether. Perhaps we'd be better off not even calling ourselves 'Christians', but simply 'People of the Way'. It would help us to avoid the mistake of thinking that what God wants us to do is set up a static group where we will feel that we are better than others; a fortress which acts as a bulwark, where we can be 'right', and others 'wrong'.

When Christians behave as though their identity is in competition with others; when they express that identity over against others, they are playing into the very logic which Jesus comes to break down. In Jesus, God gives life to all, indiscriminately. Those who respond to Jesus' call are to do the same.

'People do not change, they are merely revealed.'

ANNE ENRIGHT, WRITER

'I could believe in Jesus, if only he did not drag behind him his leprous bride, the Church.'

ATTRIBUTED TO THE POET, SHELLEY

'De-humanising others is inherently evil. As the 'Body of Christ' on earth it is our responsibility to be the light of the world and to show this for what it is, for what it does, and for how ultimately it strips us of our own humanity and Godly image as stewards of God's creation.'

SIAN NICHOLAS, READER

'There is no path; the path is made by walking.'

ANTONIO MACHADO, SPANISH POET

'It is easy to be tolerant when you do not care.'

CLEMENT F. ROGERS, THEOLOGIAN

'People pay for what they do, and still more for what they have allowed themselves to become. And they pay for it very simply: by the lives they lead.'

JAMES BALDWIN, WRITER

'There is a terrible danger in sitting inside our churches looking up in worship at our remote God in heaven, while outside the world is on fire. Worship that saves the world, on the other hand, is courageous, daring, willing to look reality in the face and step out in a way that responds to God 'doing a new thing' in his Kingdom already present with us.'

BRIAN McLAREN, THEOLOGIAN

WE ARE ONE

When Muslims go to mosque to pray, they are obliged to occupy the next available space in the row that is being filled when they enter. They are not allowed to begin their own row. They are not allowed to start a new group with their own friends. In the mosque, each one is to be treated as a friend, a brother, a sister. The social distinctions of the world outside the mosque dissolve. Because before God, everyone is equal.

Christian fellowship is like this. The presence of God bridges the distances between us.

When Jesus wanted his followers to really understand his identity and his purpose, he did not give them a theory, or explain an idea. He shared a meal with them. In that meal, which we call the Eucharist, people take on a new identity. When those around the table – whether Roman citizens and freemen or the lowest of the low, who under the law had neither freedom nor dignity – sit side by side and consume what Jesus calls his body, they all become members – limbs, or organs – of one, unified new reality. That reality is Christ.

It's easy for us to take for granted the metaphor of 'the body of Christ' (1 Corinthians 12.12–14) because we're so familiar with it. But the image is meant to convey a reality. What happens to one member, happens to all. In an organism, there is complete solidarity across all its parts. What is good for my toe, my arm, my eye, is good for me; what is bad for my toe, my arm, or my eye, is bad for me. This is what we are to one another, in Christ: different parts of the same body.

Pope Francis speaks about 'the globalization of indifference', in which we simply do not notice, and do not care, what is happening to others. But at the table of Jesus, in the body of Jesus, what happens to others really is happening to me, and vice versa. Our destiny is joined, at the deepest level. My success, my flourishing, cannot be separated from what is happening to those around me. We are all members of a single body, and so the pain of one is the pain of all. The joy of one is the joy of all.

This, in James' words, is the 'glory' of Christ, the beauty of Christ: no one is left out. No one is left behind. No one is discarded.

The question for each one of us, for each Christian community, is not whether we say we believe this. Jesus warned that what we say is not what counts (Matthew 7.21; 21.28–32). The question is whether we act in accordance with what we profess.

HUMAN IDENTITY

In Christ, there is no male or female; no Jew or Greek; no slave or free (Galatians 3.28). It has taken Christians a long time to really *hear* these words, and perhaps we still haven't. Even now, we struggle to understand and apply them. Surely Paul doesn't mean that gender, ethnicity, religion or social standing are irrelevant?

In other places in his letters, he makes clear that cultural, gender, religious and social differences are real. Paul lived in a culture which placed more emphasis on such differences than we do. Christ does not erase the differences between us. After all, human differences are good. They are what make life rich, interesting and creative and without them, humanity would not grow and flourish.

So Paul is not asking us to discard these differences. Rather, he is offering us an invitation to adopt the perspective of Christ which will allow us to see human differences in the light of the divine promise to gather all things up into a single communion of love. In Christ, that communion is already real.

Gladys Ganiel (a sociologist of religion) found that people 'are very, very critical' of the institutional Church, which they think of as the Pope and the Vatican and the bishops, but that 'most people are very pleased with their local priest'.

'It does not take much grace to be around someone who is just like you, who thinks like you, similar social class, acts like you, votes like you. Where grace is put to the test is when you are around somebody that is different to you, that thinks differently to you, who may be morally offensive to you. We do not have the option of treating that person as an outcast – as a morally offensive person.'

PHILIP YANCEY, AUTHOR

'We are walking exemplars of the 'Christ-like' life, not by our own efforts but through God's saving grace. When Christians gather at the Eucharist, they make – they are – the Church. So here come together mission and mystery.'

BISHOP STEPHEN PLATTEN

'The body of Christ is where dirt comes to be cleansed, not where the clean come to take refuge from the dirt.'

KESTER BREWIN, WRITER

'Many of us today live in a kind of inner apartheid. We segregate out a small corner of pious activity and then can make no sense out of the rest of our lives.'

RICHARD FOSTER, THEOLOGIAN

'The church's beliefs do not articulate the needs and feelings of many people in the face of the uncertainties of modern life'

MARGARET GOODALL, WRITER

'There's that hope of eternal life. I see it as though, this isn't our home, we're just passing through. That home is heaven and looking heavenwards, and so it has changed the way I think about things. It changes the way I think about life here on earth and life beyond. And there is life beyond.'

F. SIMON, CHRISTIAN

What this means for the identity wars in which our culture is currently convulsed is a matter for patient discernment. Snap judgements and easy answers are suspect. The good news about Jesus cannot be found in a series of propositions, formulae or solutions. The good news is a story of a human life, and a human death, which can never be reduced to a code for problem-solving.

But Jesus does give us a principle by which to act. Whatever we do and say, it must reflect the life-changing insight that Paul expresses so vividly. Christ is the deep truth of humanity, the fundamental identity of every human being, whatever our sex or gender, wherever we stand in the culture wars, whatever our politics, our religion, our agendas, fears, wounds and hopes. How we relate to, speak to and act towards Christ is the guide to how we should relate to, speak to and act towards everyone.

GOD HAS NO FAVOURITES

Let's go back to St Peter's and my own startled discovery that 'God is no respecter of persons'. The full force of this odd expression should now be clear. God does not discriminate between people on the basis of their social class, standing, position, history or perceived importance. Why? Not, as I anxiously wondered standing there in the church that afternoon, because *God doesn't 'respect' anyone*, but quite the opposite: because *God respects everyone*. 'God has no favourites', not because God doesn't favour anyone, but because *God favours everyone*.

Every single human being, of whatever age, sex, class, race, or religion, is in God's image. Jesus has identified himself personally with each one.

Peter had assumed, approaching the Roman centurion Cornelius, that God couldn't possibly favour this man because he was a pagan, a soldier, an oppressor (Acts 10. 28). What he discovered, by watching the way God accepted Cornelius, was that God accepts people from 'every nation' equally: from every different social group, including those who, for one reason or another, our own group might have reason to dislike or exclude. God's love is not selective. It does not discriminate between ethnicities, nationalities, socioeconomic or religious identities. The Holy Spirit, Peter was forced to admit, was just as eager to pour out his gifts on Cornelius as on himself.

Every Christian is called to make the same discovery as Peter. Each of us is called to recognize again and again that God does not share our desire to exclude. He does not apportion his welcome and his love according to our prejudices. He does not draw boundaries around 'the some' and exclude 'the other'. These is absolutely no doubt that God has no favourites, because God favours everyone.

'The greatest barrier to the gospel in contemporary Western culture is the church.'

MICHAEL RIDDELL, AUTHOR

'The church must be the first sign of what it preaches.'

FR MICHAEL CROSBY

SESSION 5
WHAT IS A CHRISTIAN?

1. Brother Roger of Taizé said, 'Jesus did not come to found a religion. He came to give people life.' Does your community 'give life'? How might it give life more abundantly, more widely?

2. Revisit p. 28 and Track 19 of the course audio/transcript. What do you think of the Muslim obligation to fill the seats in a mosque in strict order? Can you imagine the effect this might have in your own church? Perhaps new friendships would blossom and lonely people feel more included . . ?

3. Track 18. What difference would it make if Christians thought of themselves as 'People of the Way'?

4. Why do you think, after more than 2,000 years, that we still find it so difficult to grasp that 'God's love is not selective. It does not discriminate between ethnicities, nationalities, socioeconomic or religious identities'?

5. Read the words of Anne Enright on p. 27. ('People do not change, they are merely revealed.') Discuss, in the light of your experience and your Christian faith.

6. Revisit Track 18. These days it's mainstream to be secular rather than Christian – or indeed any other religion. Like Frances, do you ever feel embarrassed to own up to the fact that you go to church? Does it put a barrier between you and other people, do you think?

7. Revisit Track 19. Conventions in churches have become more relaxed: no dress code; a more welcoming place for children; fun and laughter allowed. To encourage people inside, Norwich Cathedral even erected a helter-skelter indoors in 2019, as a fun way to view their medieval roof. Share your opinions and experiences of such changes.

8. Carmody reminds us of Jesus' warning that it is not what we say, but what we do, that counts (Matthew 7.21; 21.28–32). How do you live with the gap between your Christian ideals and the messy reality of your life?

9. From your own understanding of Jesus, do you feel he would have been for or against gay marriage?

10. On Track 20, Carmody talks of her Christian faith/journey as 'going on an adventure'. Does that resonate with you?

CARMODY GREY is Assistant Professor of Catholic Theology at Durham University, and has degrees in theology from Trinity College Oxford, King's College Cambridge and the University of Nottingham. She teaches and speaks publicly in a variety of arenas, is a columnist for *The Tablet*, and sits on the Advisory Board of Las Casas Institute (Blackfriars Hall, Oxford).

SIMON STANLEY is co-founder of York Courses, a Canon Emeritus of York Minster and a former BBC producer/presenter.

OUR WARM THANKS to Gavin Mist for recording and producing the course audio. Photography © Getty Images.

York Courses: **spckpublishing.co.uk/bible-studies-and-group-resources/york-courses**

A FIVE-SESSION COURSE FOR
DISCUSSION GROUPS AND INDIVIDUALS
SUITABLE FOR LENT OR ANY SEASON

FIVE SESSIONS
1 THE BEST PICTURE OF GOD | 2 NEITHER JEW NOR GENTILE | 3 NEITHER MALE NOR FEMALE
4 NEITHER SLAVE NOR FREE | 5 WHAT IS A CHRISTIAN?

'Accessibly weaves substantial theology with Bible study, emphasizing that we need to unfamiliarize ourselves with the Bible, letting its sheer strangeness jolt us. Plenty of personal glimpses and fascinating detail include an Orthodox priest protesting that a prostitute is not a sinner, but an icon in the dustbin . . .'
DAVID WILBOURNE, *CHURCH TIMES*

THE COURSE BOOKLET is written by Carmody Grey. Each of the five sessions ends with a range of questions designed to stimulate lively group discussion. Ideally each group member should have a personal copy.

THE COURSE AUDIO contains a relaxed conversation between Carmody Grey and Simon Stanley, exploring and expanding on topics raised in the course booklet, with contributions from three people from different Christian backgrounds.

THE COURSE TRANSCRIPT BOOKLET is a complete record of the words spoken on the audio and includes CD track numbers. Especially useful for group leaders as they prepare, it can also help group members to catch up on anything they've missed; to go over the recorded material at leisure; and to feel more confident about joining in the discussion.

The audio material and course booklet work hand in hand with each other and both are essential for following the development of the themes raised in this course.

Christian Living
eBook available

ISBN 978-1-909107-33-5

9 781909 107335

Scan to find out more

Cover photograph © Getty Images

 spck.org.uk
 @SPCKPublishing
 /SPCKPublishing
 @SPCK_Publishing

 spck

 YORK COURSES